THE PRINCIPLES OF ORTHODOX ASCESIS AND MONASTICISM

by Archimandrite Sophronios Essex

In every era we find the human spirit preoccupied with the issue of ascesis[1]. Ascesis is a matter of principal significance, not only for those who embarked on becoming ascetic in the narrow meaning of monks and hermits only for example, but generally for every Christian. Ascesis, understood as spiritual labor, is an integral part of the history of all known religions and civilizations, even those civilizations that do not have a religious foundation. Every religion, all the old and novel secular creeds, the lives of the mystics, they all contain their ascetic education which varies according to their underlying doctrinal awareness. (The dependence of the ascetic practice on the form of the doctrinal awareness and, vice versa, the dependence of the teaching on the spiritual experience, is a matter of great interest, that I am attempting to present in this short writing on the Orthodox ascesis.)

For us Christ is absolute truth: He is God. Creator and God-Savior. His commandments are the Uncreated Light of deity. The essence of Orthodox ascesis is found in our effort to make these commandments into the comprehensive law of the entirety of our temporal and eternal existence. The ascetic is constantly trying to reach perfection. But, the perfection we have in mind is not to be found in the created nature of man and so cannot be achieved by developing the capacities of this nature, as it is with its limitations. Perfection is found in the Divine

---

[1] Definition of Ascesis to be used throughout this book: the practice of severe self-discipline, typically for religious reasons.

Being, and it is a gift of the Holy Spirit. From this follows that the ascetic concentrates on an effort to unite his life and will, with the life and will of God Himself. This he achieves mainly through prayer, and prayer is the pinnacle of every ascetic activity. The Orthodox ascesis reaches its loftiest expression through prayer, and the Orthodox ascetic devotes his main activities to prayer. Since prayer is a wonderfully creative act, it is capable of infinite diversity, as much in its forms as in its efficacy. The most perfect type of prayer is known as the "pure prayer", through which we enter the Divine Being through the power of the Holy Spirit. This is the final purpose of true ascesis. For this purpose the ascetic sets everything aside. Among others, the monastic renunciation of the world is included in this setting everything aside.

We should now shift our attention to the examination of monasticism, this would not signify any confinement of our topic. Monasticism is not a profession that differs from the faith of other Christians. It is merely another form of life, that stems however from those same commandments of Christ, the practical implementation of which certainly entails ascetic effort. Wherever a Christian resides, there too must exist ascetic practice, and so, when we speak of monastic ascesis we are referring to something that is familiar and close to every Orthodox believer.

The renunciation of the world and the commitment required by the monk are not always easily understood. Is it possible to base a full, authentic life on a denial, on the principles of renunciation? This, more or less, is the widespread reaction. The answer is: Of course not. Christ's commandments and mainly, love, are positive by their nature, and in general, life according to God can only exist as a positive act. When there is love for God, there is no need for exerting effort, in the form of self-denial, for one to conquer this or that passion. He who is full of love for Christ, he for whom this love has become a second nature, needs not reject the dependence on the worldly things nor his enslavement to passions, for he is already free of them. In this state of love, every spiritual act that is performed according to Christ's commandments is the spontaneous, full of gratitude, expression of love, not the result of any coercion upon himself. But because of the fall of man, the positive energy according to the commandments of the Gospel, that is the ceaseless continuity and growth in the love of God, is unavoidably connected in this life with ascesis in its negative aspect, that is with the resistance to the law of sin to which we are enslaved. The whole world lies in the power of the evil one, says Saint John the Theologian. Evil is the fact that we have become enslaved to sin. The liberation of man, who is free in his original nature, his rebirth into eternal divine life, the transformation and the sanctification of his entire existence, stems from the unification of the divine with the human. In the human field it is the negative energy that dominates, while in the divine it is always the positive that prevails.

The concept that the world must be renounced has led the majority of people to consider the monastic society as something melancholic and sad. But those who have chosen monasticism, view it differently. Saint Theodore the Studite for example, driven by his enthusiasm for monastic life, called it the third grace. The first grace was the Law of Moses, the second, the grace upon grace which we have all received from the fullness of Christ, and now the third, the monastic life, understood as the heavenly life, as the angelic world descends upon earth, as the achievement and realization in history of that which, by its essence, lies beyond the boundaries of history.

Bishop Ignatius Brianchaninov who was distinguished in the rich flourishing of the Russian Church during the 19th century, has this to say about monastic life: Christian perfection consists of a pure heart to which God appears and to which he reveals his presence through the various gifts of the Holy Spirit. He who has reached such perfection becomes a bearer of light and fulfills the commandment for loving thy neighbor, not by some material service, but with the service of the Spirit, leading those who seek salvation, lifting them when they fall, and healing their wounded souls. The chorus of monks has delivered to the Church of Christ shepherds who, by accompanying their teaching with miracles, have preserved and enshrined these, not in words of human wisdom, but in words they have been taught by the Spirit.

Here is why we see the Church resorting to the desert, following the era of the martyrs. This is where its perfection resorted to, there in the desert its source of light lived. There we find the true strength of the Church militant. What were John the Chrysostom, Basil the Great, Epifanios, the Metropolitans Alexios and Philip, and what were all the holy (saint) shepherds? Such bearers of light are found not only among the rank of bishops, but also among the simple monks, from Anthony the Great and Saint John of Damascus, to Sergio of Rantonez and George the Anchorite. They are the ones who anchored the faith, and denounced and overturned heresy. Without monastics, wouldn't Christianity have been erased off the earth? This is why perfection is so essential to the Christian Church. Without this, even salvation and faith can easily vanquish, and would surely vanquish. Because there needs to be senses exercised to discern both good and evil (Hebrews 5:14). In the first Church it was ascetics and martyrs who achieved such perfection; after them it was the monastics.

What an arrogant statement about monastic life! You may say! What a proud heart it reveals! Filth goes unnoticed in a dark room, we answer, while in a room lit by the shining rays of the sun, even the tinniest molecule of dust is revealed. The Holy Spirit teaches humility. When it establishes its residence in the heart, it inspires in us sighs unfathomable by the human tongue and it declares to man the nullity of his justice, in the words of Isaiah: All our righteous deeds are like a menstrual rag (Isaiah 64:6). True diabolic pride is to ignore the gift of God as if it never existed.

If we wished to maintain zeal for perfection, which has been commanded to us by Christ, be perfect, therefore, as your heavenly Father is perfect (Matthew 5:48), we should not lose sight of the perception of the Holy Fathers about the monastic life. Indeed, were we to let our attention indulge only into the exterior daily life of the Church, we might easily get discouraged, even scandalized. But, if we study the Church in its essence and in the divine life that it delivers us, no external condition, however difficult and unpleasant it happens to be, can distance us from the love of Christ. In the words of prophet David, great peace have they which love thy law and nothing shall offend them (Psalms 118:165).

Lets now move on to the study of this monasticism, studying, in sequence, the three ways of the calling, the three renunciations, the three aspects of the cross and the three degrees of monastic devotion.

Minor differences in interpretation over this or that point may be observed among the ascetics, since the full acceptance of the teachings and traditions of the Church does not exclude variations over nonessential issues. For example, on Mount Athos, especially among the anchorites who live in small communities and in hermitage and even in monasteries, although this is more rare, there is the tendency for the immediate vestment with the great schema. The novice makes his vows and is immediately vested with the great schema, of the decision made once and for all. But, in the broader experience of the Church, we find the tradition of the three grades of monasticism: the novice (wearing of the habit without having made vows), the small schema and the great schema. These three grades of the monastic society correspond to the three renunciations that were used by the Holy Fathers and particularly by Saint John the Cassian and Saint John Climacus.

The Cassian writes: There are three types of calling, thus we consider three renunciations necessary for the monastic, whichever their way of calling may be. According to Cassian, the first type of calling is the direct call from God. The second takes place through the mediation of people, and the third through necessity. A degree of inspiration is a characteristic of the first kind of calling. The heart is inspired even in sleep and is drawn without restraint towards the love of God and the commandments of Christ.

The second kind, the one from people, happens when someone is aflame with desire for God by the words or the influence of holy people. The third kind, the one out of necessity, comes from incidents like material misfortune, sickness, or the loss of loved ones that can motivate a person to turn to God.

In the teachings of the Holy Fathers I could add one or two observations I gathered during my spiritual communication with multiple ascetics at Mount Athos. There are people raised inside the church, whose souls mature slowly in the atmosphere of its ancient traditions, its majestic service, its sacramental life, as well as through the never-ending liturgical and dogmatic treasures, by the power of which elation and peace are born inside of them; they are not subjected to acute crises or violent shifts. Sometimes they experience from their childhoods a deep and powerful aptitude towards God which finally becomes more important than anything else and brings them in a simple and natural way, to the monastery. The situation is completely different for those who have lost God for another reason, have abandoned God, or are "separated" from God by their own will. Their "return" in general, takes the form of an acute internal crisis that rips them apart and shakes them to their core. They usually fall victim of various neurological issues and other pathological abnormalities; might even drive them to insanity. The spiritual rebirth of these people, who have often fallen really low in every aspect, happens under the experience of the energy of Grace, which they actually feel. Grace which introduces us to the world of the Divine light, despite its gravitational power does not strip us from our freedom of will, neither relieves us from future struggle or even from doubts and hesitations. Those who have experienced this Grace might even submit to temptation, possibly in a demonic darkness, and then the knowledge that has been given to them and has undoubtedly made a significant impression to their mental[2] consciousness, might be put to the service of evil. "And the final condition of that person is worse than the first." (Mat.12 45). At some point though and despite all of the above, Grace flows so abundantly that the soul is fully aware of its resurrection. The internal testimony of the Spirit towards the truth is so clear, there is no room left for doubts or hesitations. Love for God fills

[2] Νοητική or nous in English.

and dominates their entire existence. When this happens, the soul is solidified for the rest of its existence, and receives freedom from internal struggles to its full extent. No more painful search for the truth. From now on, all of its efforts will be directed towards realizing what was revealed during the time of the "divine visitation".

Before we leave this question behind us, allow me to add that the Holy Fathers never underestimated any form of calling because the history of the church includes many incidents of people reaching their calling through their needs and achieving greater perfection from those called directly by God. Hence, the Fathers evaluated not from the beginning but from the end of the road one reached.

There is some analogy correspondence between the three types of callings, the three renunciations, as well as the three ranks of monastic devotion. Cassian classifies the three renunciations in the following order: 1) Denial of wealth and possessions of this world, 2) denial of passions and past habits, both material and immaterial, and 3) the type of denial where the mind is detached from all visible and temporary things and is submerged into the contemplation of the invisible and the eternal. "These 3 denials are essential if we want to achieve perfection", says Cassian.

Now let's stop and let's study the teachings of another prominent teacher of eastern monasticism, Saint John Climacus who writes the following: "No one shall enter the celestial palace wearing a crown, unless they have fulfilled the first, the second, and the third renunciation. The first renunciation is the renunciation of all things, of the world and of relatives. The second is the renunciation of 'our selfish will'. And the third, the renunciation of vanity, following close upon obedience[3]."

Now, if we compare the teachings of those two Saints, it would initially seem as if the three forms of renunciation suggested by them, do not match. While Saint John begins by demanding the renunciation of the world without exception, Cassian includes the renunciation of one's parents into the second kind, the one that includes abandoning old habits, old ways of thinking, moral behavior, and passions in general. Saint John places the denial of our "selfish will" in the second kind, and last of all, according to him, comes the rejection of vanity. I would like to point out here though, the stunning unity in spirit and tradition of the two Fathers despite their differences in expression, coming as a result of their different personal experiences. The only divergence is found in the extent (scope) of the first renunciation. According to Cassian, it is enough for the candidate to abandon the outside world and material possessions. Saint John on the other hand, demands from the beginning the renunciation of all human bonds; otherwise, the abdication of everything worldly is uncertain. After all that, meaning the second form of renunciation, he speaks about the struggle against passions in terms that lead straight to the root of the problem. In that, lies the superiority of

---

[3] Meaning vanity follows closely after obedience.

his conceptualization. In his third form of renunciation, Saint John is again more perfect despite the fact that the content is the same to that of Cassian. The latter speaks about separation of the mind from all visible things in favor of the deeper study of the invisible and the eternal. Yet, to the soul not clean of passion, this instruction might direct the imagination to start working, since "the invisible and the eternal" are still, as one would say, outside of us and our reach. So, the "rejection of vanity" process of Saint John introduces the ascetic to the core of the internal struggle and forces the mind to remain composed and aware, instead of wondering into "higher spheres" until the end.

Although I have allowed myself to express an opinion saying that the three forms of renunciation by Saint John are superior to those of Cassian both ascetically and pedagogically, I must repeat that both processes are the same. Allow me to explain.

The rejection of vanity from Saint John is nothing more that the ascetic instruction to transfer our spirit to the eternal world. This is what declares our victory over the world we live in. But who is the one that triumphs in this world we live in? The Church recognizes a category of Saints the "Fools for Christ" whose spiritual exploits are an especially glorious expression of the third level of renunciation. The purpose of the "Fools" is to make themselves be despised by people. There are many people who don't understand this idea. They view it as a form of perversion, although in reality it is the best way to avoid vanity and thus the way to win a victory over this world. “Don’t you want to come to me to have life?” said the Lord. “I don’t receive glory from people. But I made known to you that you don’t have inside you the love of God … how can you believe, you who take glory from each other, and don’t ask that glory only from God?” (John 5:40-44). So, for one to accept honor from people is a hurdle in the way even for faith. But, if we follow the instruction of Saint John in our lives in order to renounce vanity, we will see that this renunciation surely makes people capable of transferring themselves mentally[4] and spiritually from this world, to the divine One. The psalm shows another way: “I would move away from this place and go reside in the desert” (Psalm 54’ 8). Apostle Paul also says: “Because who do I convince now, people, or God? Or do I ask to be liked by people? Because if I was still to be liked by people, I wouldn’t be a servant of Christ” (Gal, 1:10). And he continues: “But brothers I make known to you that the Gospel preached by me is not according to man, because neither have I received it by a man, nor it has been taught to me, but through revelation from Jesus Christ” (Gal. 1:11). So, if this Gospel is not “from man”, and is not taught by man, the third renunciation of Saint John referring to vanity must without a doubt be a road leading the spirit straight to the Divine world.

Since every renunciation coincides with teachings about accepting a cross, there are three crosses for our three renunciations. The Holy Fathers

---

[4] Νοητικά derived from nous but this does not translate to English well.

provide us with very strict warnings that the cross we will bear must be proportionate to our strength. We shall be punished severely if we risk prematurely with the third cross of the ultimate renunciation. (By "prematurely" I mean without having adequate knowledge or, better, experience; without being in the appropriate spiritual state). The one who after reading the lives of the Holy Fathers proudly wishes vividly the heights of pure, clean prayer without first having achieved success in the lower levels, will pitifully fall down to earth. Isaac of Nineveh has spoken about this concept with particular fortitude, as did another great ascetic and theologian, Bishop Theofanis the Enclosed[5]. In a remarkable essay of his titled: "The three crosses", he points out that the first cross consists of sorrows and mischiefs falling upon us people during our earthly lives; the second is our inner struggle, our passions, and our desires, and the third is the one of full surrender to God's will. This third one is according to Theofanis the consequence of the Holy Spirit's grace, which in its full form belongs only to the perfect ones. Here we meet again a different expression, although the content and the spirit are the same. In any case, let's not stop now to declare that full submission to God's will is nothing more than the third renunciation; let's instead move on to a study of the three ranks as well as the three basic promises of monasticism.

We have already said that the candidate monastic makes no promises when first wearing the monastic garments. In the Greek monasteries of

---

[5] Θεοφάνης ο Έγκλειστος

Mount Athos, this first level is considered more as a blessing which provides the right of wearing the monastic attire; hence the term "man of the cloth". Before that, the candidate is introduced to the meaning of monasticism and the need to renounce the world, as well as all relatives. Yet, since no promises have been made so far, this phase is in reality a period of testing during which the candidate is prepared for the spiritual fight.

The second level is the "Small Schema", when the monk enunciates promises that will be repeated slightly differently when he ascends to the higher level of monasticism, the "Great Schema" or as it's generally known, the "Schema".

To make the three basic promises all at once and not successively, might seem as contradicting the order and structure of renunciations described above. But the contradiction is only superficial and does not affect the essence, even the least. As with the three renunciations, it's a case of steady progress towards spiritual knowledge since all three promises have one unique goal. Their repetition during the "Small Schema" as well as during the "Great Schema" is a point not of temporary nature, but a point of increase towards the knowledge of their power and significance. There might be only a small exterior difference between the two, but a deep change might have taken place inside the monastics' internal awareness. In order not to lose the essence of the spiritual Christian life from right in front of us, allow me to stress out again that all these orders of dedication, tonsure, and promises are not the only way to reach perfection of divine love, which can be achieved also outside the monastic state. But, as the evangelist Luke spoke about Christ and said that He "was growing and His spirit was strengthening" (Luke, 1:80), so must we all develop and increase, and the experience of the Church has proven the value of monasticism many times. Apostle Peter wrote: "That's why my brothers try even more to secure being called and chosen by God. Because if you apply the above, you shall never falter; this way you shall be granted generously entrance to the eternal kingdom of our Lord and savior Jesus Christ" (B' Peter, 1:10-11).

These are the questions the candidate for the "Small Schema" is asked:

> (1) "Will you remain in the Monastery and in ascesis up to your last breath?"
>
> (2) "Will you preserve yourself in virginity and chastity and piety?"
>
> (3) "Will you preserve unto death obedience to the Superior[6], and to the whole Brotherhood in Christ?"
>
> (4) "Will you endure every affliction and deprivation of the monastic life for the sake of the Kingdom of Heaven?"

For the "Great Schema" we have the following:

[6] Abbot or Abbess of the monastery.

(1) “Do you renounce the world and the things which are in the world, according to the commandment of the Lord?”

(2) “Will you remain in the Monastery and in ascesis up to your last breath?”

(3) “Will you preserve unto death obedience to the Superior, and to the whole Brotherhood in Christ?”

(4) “Will you endure every affliction and deprivation of the Monastic life for the sake of the Kingdom of Heaven?”

(5) “Will you preserve yourself in virginity and chastity and piety?”

For each one of these questions the monk answers: “Yes, with the help of God”.

But one can ask here, if four promises are made during the “Small Schema” and five during the “Great Schema", why do we talk about three renunciations? The tradition of the Church condenses the essence of monastic tonsure into the three promises of obedience, chastity, and devotion to the spirit of poverty. We shall follow this order without examining for the time being the details of this issue which becomes more complicated if we examine separately the content of the two services. During the tonsure, the words of the abbot towards the candidate reveal suggestions for other “deeds”. “And indeed a monastic you have become before all, cleanse yourself from all that infect the flesh and the spirit, acquire humility, repel the audacity of emotive habit, be patient through praying, do not abandon fasting, do not be sluggard during the night vigils", all those summarized in the three promises of obedience, chastity, and poverty. The abbot continues: "You must, when you take the path leading to the Kingdom of Heaven, not turn back, because you will not be worthy to enter the Kingdom of Heaven. Don't favor anything else before God; do not love mother, father, siblings, or yourself, nor love yourself more than God, or the kingdoms of this world or any sort of rest and honor". During the tonsure of the "Great Schema" even bigger emphasis is given to the renunciation of the world. "Thus, the renunciation" the abbot explains, "is nothing more than a promise of crucifixion and death. So, know that from this day forward you are crucified and dead to the world through perfect renunciation; you renounce parents, siblings, wives, offspring, fathers, relatives, friends, habits, the noises of the world, cares, possessions, existence, the empty and vain glory, and you renounce not only the previously mentioned but even your own soul as the Lord says: "Those who want to come with me, renounce yourself, lift your cross and follow Me". So, if you follow Him in order to serve Him, and if you long to be called to serve as His disciple, prepare yourself from now; for spiritual fights, for temperance of flesh, for cleansing of your soul, for paltry poverty, for benevolent grief, for all the sad and painful instances one will experience inside the joyous life close to God; to be hungry and thirsty and naked, be insulted and mocked, be disgraced, persecuted, and much more. And when all these happen to you be glad, your fame and your value are high in heaven. Be joyful and jubilant for today the Lord our God has chosen you and separated you from life mortal, and placed you in the camp of the angelic life. Up there, be a servant, take part in things, seek them, as our government exists in heaven, according to the Apostle. Oh, the new call! Oh, the gift of Mystery! Second baptism[7] you receive today brother, the fortune of our Merciful God's grants, and your sins (God) cleanses, and you become a child of light, and He, Christ our Lord congratulates you through His holy angels for your penance, sacrificing for you the fattened calf " After that, the monastic is asked to "walk worthy of his calling" and is given certain instructions regarding ascetic life which is the expression of the steps he has just taken.

At first, when we hear of this process, its true meaning is not obvious to us. We only partly understand or deduce that, for which the person has been called for. Because only experience, a genuine, honest experience can reveal the true content and power of these words. We do not deny that the invitation to renounce the love towards relatives and the world to the monastic in general, and live in the image of Christ can cause a deep internal division of

---

[7] The expression "second baptism" declares that the attire of the monastic with its grandeur and the abundance of the Grace of the Holy Spirit that has flown to the monastic are similar to the mystery of baptism, which as such in the Orthodox Symbol of faith always remains "one" (I acknowledge one baptism for the remission of sins.) and non-repeatable.

the soul, or to use modern terms, a "complex". The soul is swept by great storms and whoever is left alone without the guidance coming from the thousands of years of the Church's experience, is not just facing the possibility of hardships, but also the possibility to be lost completely. In "The Ladder of Divine Ascent" which is one of the most prominent works dealing with ascetic practice, Saint John writes: "It is vital for the sea[8], to move and be rough, be agitated and enraged, so that the storms and the blizzards throw to the land all the decay and rot that the rivers of the sufferings have dropped into it. If we look carefully, we will see that the sea storms are followed by a deep tranquility".

It's hard for one to find words to describe the need for the push of this internal conflict towards its extreme limits, in order to reveal the depths of the soul. How can we prove with words that its necessary for our spirit to reside both in hades and with God? How can anyone explain that it's the only way we can achieve the fulfillment of human life, and at the same time the balance in spirit that nullifies all internal imbalances? Who among us isn't familiar with those painful changes of spiritual elevation and fall? But, when one descends to the abyss of our internal struggles and brings God to him, by this "achievement" alone, one can avoid all these pathological ambivalences of elevation and fall we always hear about, because he carries the Whole inside of him. We have the commandment from

---

[8] By the word 'sea' Saint John Climacus here means the spiritual life of the individual.

Christ to be like God, a life which the Fathers call "science of all sciences" and "art of all arts" and the only way to acquire its knowledge is only through experience.

Now, how can all these "harsh" words we find in the discussion of making these promises, be compatible to "life in the image of Christ"? Where is the meekness and the love the Lord is calling us towards? The spiritual perspective is vastly different from the "psychological" one. Try to define the common perception people have for example about sanctity, love, or meekness and you will realize it barely corresponds to the perception of it inside the Gospels. Many people understand meekness as a by nature peaceful disposition. Saint John Climacus offers a different interpretation[9]. "Meekness he says, is that state of intellect that holds a person unshakable, both in the presence of honor and disgrace. Meekness is a rock immovable standing above a sea of insanity, the confirmation of patience, the entrance towards, as well as the mother of love, the safety in praying, the temple of the Holy Spirit, the curbing of violence, the fountain of happiness, the mimicking of Christ". From this we observe that meekness is something immeasurably greater than any "psychological" disposition. Meekness is the courage one develops to carry the burdens and the weaknesses of others. It is the steady readiness one has to endure defamation and stay imperturbable to

---

[9] As far as meekness, simplicity and brevity are concerned that do not coming naturally but have been acquired through pains and struggles.

praise. Meekness is the quiet solution in the face of every sorrow, even in death. Meekness encapsulates great power in itself and victory upon the world. Christ says: "Blessed are the meek for they shall inherit the earth". Meaning, they will conquer and overpower "the world" in the highest sense of the term. The world shall submit, not to a brutal material force, but to meekness.

Since we digressed to present the general image of the essence and the spirit of monasticism, let's proceed to examine in detail each one of the three basic promises.

Many believe that the main difference between monasticism and the lives of ordinary people can be found in celibacy, demanded from both monks and nuns. But, according to the Holy Fathers as well as the ascetics of modern day, I would place more emphasis on obedience, because we often see ordinary people spend their lives unmarried, without becoming monks or nuns; neither in the mystic sense, nor in spirit. Likewise, poverty in the sense of one being satisfied with very little can also be found in people very distant to the monastic spirit. Despite all that though, it's not in my intentions to try and establish a ranking of the three basic promises. I rather hope to show that it is the combination of the three as a whole, that creates conditions helping the ascetic in his or her main purpose; freedom from passion, and pure prayer.

Obedience is the base of monasticism but it's hard to talk about it, as it appears to begin by taking crude and naïve forms, yet, it leads the person later towards a world impossible to describe since no human meaning can explain it. Obedience is a mystery only revealed by the Holy Spirit. And obedience is both "life within the Church" and a mystery, indeed. At first, resignation of free will and power of logic could seem like going against God's plan for people, as they have been endowed with freedom matching the freedom of God and are invited by this freedom to rein eternally. Placing their freedom and free will in the hands of someone else even if that other person is a priest could cause many people the feeling of losing the ground under their feet. Such a step would seem to them as if they injected themselves into a black abyss, that they would lose their personality surrendering themselves to the worst possible slavery. It would be an auto-cancellation. Yet, for those who have followed by faith the teachings of the Church and have denied themselves according to the spirit of those teachings, obedience is revealed as an indescribable great gift "from above". The person of obedience can be compared to the eagle that lifts to the sky by its strong wings and there peacefully measures the distance that separates it from the ground; enjoying its safety and dominion over heights unreachable and deadly terrifying to others. With trust, love, and joy, the candidate[10] ascetics willingly submit their will and judgment to their spiritual fathers, and by doing that, they are relieved from the heavy burden of earthly

[10] The term candidate applies not only to the candidate monastic, but also to any monastic and Christian that turns to their spiritual father for guidance.

cares and reach to something invaluable, the "by God" clarity of the mind.

Monasticism means above all a "pure[11] nous", impossible without obedience. This is the reason why there can be no monasticism without obedience, and the person who is not obedient can never be a monk or a nun in the true meaning of the word. It is possible for one to receive great gifts from God, even the perfection of martyrdom, outside monasticism. The "pure nous" though is a special gift to monasticism, unknown to all the other paths and the only way a monk can reach this state is through obedience. This is why I consider obedience to be the main foundation of monasticism that includes the other two promises as naturally complimentary. Saint John Climacus for example says: "The mother of purity is the eternal silence[12] and obedience. The freedom from passions acquired through internal silence cannot remain unmoved when in constant contact with the outside world. But, when this freedom is born out of obedience it is in all instances prudent and unshakable". And for poverty he says: "Can the one who surrendered his soul still have the desire of ownership?" So, obedience through the "departure from the world and the alienation from personal will", "with golden wings ascends tirelessly towards the sky of freedom from passion".

Obedience is a mystery of the Church, thus,

---

[11] As in clean.

[12] Stillness.

the relationship between the elder[13] the candidate is of a divine nature. We have already emphasised that this mystery exists for the candidate to learn to perform the will of God, to enter the sphere of the divine will, and by that to become a member of the divine life. For the elder, the mystery means that through their prayer and life of spiritual effort, they shall bring the candidate to the knowledge of that life, and help them develop internally true freedom, without which salvation is impossible. "Where the spirit of the Lord is, there is also freedom" (2 Kor. 3:17). So, the purpose of obedience like the purpose of Christian life in general is to acquire the Holy Spirit.

A spiritual guide must never try to submit the will of the candidate to his own "human" will, but, through the course of everyday life he could find himself to be forced to insist in executing his instructions; a situation no obedient candidate would wish to drive his elder into.

Because of his great responsibility towards God, the ascetic effort necessary for the elder is much heavier than the one required by the candidate. But, his responsibility exists only if the candidate shows complete obedience. When this doesn't happen, the candidate carries the whole weight of his actions and loses the benefits of obedience. In any case, the institution of "the elder" does not exist to relieve the

---

[13] Elder –'starets' in Russian, senior (Mat. 15:2, Mark 7:3), a monastic distinguished for their sanctity, long experience in the spiritual life, and the gift of guiding souls.

candidate from responsibility, but to teach him the true Christian life and the true Christian freedom, for which one must overcome himself through the spiritual accomplishment of obedience, the passions of ambition and love for power. Whoever asks to enslave his brother or fellow human or even to abuse his freedom is unavoidably destroying his own freedom also, as this act of such violation of another person's freedom constitutes a fall from the divine life of love towards which we have been summoned.

One of the main obstacles preventing us from reaching the condition, towards which we have been called via the commands by Christ, is love towards ourselves, our selfishness. Obedience is the best way to overcome this consequence of the original sin inside of us. When we deny our own will and we accept the will of our brother, we overcome the "division" that was introduced to our nature from the fall of Adam, which was one, originally. Where does this conflict of wills inside of us, come from? Isn't there only one will of God?

When we "despise" our little "individual" wishes and "remove" our will in front of God by surrendering to Him, we become worthy of accepting and carrying inside of us the energy of the Divine Will. When we perfect our obedience towards God and our brother, we perfect towards love, we expand our existence, until we reach the completeness of the God-man existence in the image of Christ. Because, there is no limit to the love of God for us, and despite the fact that in His essence God remains and will eternally remain unreachable and incomprehensible to us, by Divine energy and grace God wishes to bond with us so closely, so fully, that man can become by grace, god; like the God Creator, in the image of God's existence. The Book of Revelations mentions: "To the one who is victorious, I will give the right to sit with me on my throne, just as I was victorious and sat down with my Father on His throne." (Rev. 3:21).

The educated person of the modern era with a developed critical approach is immeasurably less adept to the ascetic application of obedience than the simple one who is not affected by intellectual curiosity. The educated person, in love with his own intellect, which he's used to consider as the only stable foundation of his "personal" life, must renounce this wealth of his before becoming a monastic; otherwise it will be very difficult for them "to enter the Kingdom" (Luke 14:33). But how will this happen? Isn't the person in whose hands we must put our will into, just another person like us, someone who in reality might on occasion appear to be inferior? The candidate starts discussing with himself: "So, this elder is an oracle? How does he know the will of God? God has given us reason and we must think on our own. For example, what the elder just said makes no sense. It's totally irrational". And so on. This type of stance fills the candidate with doubt and hesitation against every word coming from his spiritual father, for every instruction he receives from him. He then forgets that the divine will in this world is revealed by using the exact same external forms that are used to manifest the natural will of the person, as well as the demonic will when the latter manifests through people. He judges by external appearances based on the ways of the "logical" person and he can't find the way leading to the living faith.

Saint John Climacus says that the monk who "willingly submits to servitude, receives true freedom in return". That's why in the end as it happens, the experience of obedience becomes an experience of true freedom "in God".

In the presence of divine truth, the monk is completely persuaded of the imperfection of his powers of reasoning. This constitutes an important phase of the ascetic life. By doubting his intellect, the monk is freed from the nightmare in which the whole of humankind lives in.

There are two categories of monks: Those who possess the gift of simple, direct faith and for that reason it's easy for them to enter the road of true obedience, and those who despite their fiery desire for God as well as their burning desire to live according to the commandments of the Lord, face great difficulties when they try to rid themselves of their self-confidence in order to learn obedience. When the monk, filled with faith towards God, his protector, as well as with trust in his spiritual father abandons his own individual will and judgment, the depths of his esoteric experience persuade him joyfully that he has reached "a spring of water welling up to eternal life." (John 4:14).

With this renunciation of will and judgment in favor of the attachment to God's will which surpasses all human wisdom, the monastic in reality renounces nothing more than his own egocentric will, which is the result of passions as well as of his own weak and limited intellect; by doing that he shows true wisdom and superior will. By this way the monastic is, in a way that is incomprehensible even to him/her walking towards a height that people possessing the highest intellect cannot reach, or even comprehend. This height is "by God the pure nous" as we have previously mentioned. Obedience is the road of the faith, the one that was "victorious over the world" (A' John 5:4). Yet, not all can conceive this mystery. In one of his letters, Bishop Ignatius Brianchianinov writes: "We believe as the Holy Fathers have taught us, that if the Lord Himself does not teach the road to obedience, the monastic cannot learn anything from people. And even if the Holy Apostles appeared in front of him, he could have thrown stones at them".

Monastic obedience is not "discipline". Today, the existence of all human institutions or societies depends on the modulation of the activities of their members. And this modulation is achieved by discipline which is based on the submission of the will of the inferior to the one of the superior, or the "majority". Such obedience is usually enforced under compulsion. But, even when we have willingly and logically an acceptance of discipline as an essential state necessary to the continuous existence of a community, discipline is still discipline since its foundational principal is the submission of the will of a person to that of another.

Monastic obedience on the other hand, is a religious act and as such, one must freely give consent, otherwise it loses its religious significance. Such obedience can become spiritually fruitful only when it carries the characteristic of voluntary submission of the will and judgment to that of someone else, in order to reach the will of God. It is that relation between obedience and the search of divine will that helps us find the essence of our own obedience.

The monk recognizes his own inability to discover God's will on his own so he turns to his spiritual father who he believes him to be more worthy to know the will of God. The elder doesn't try to destroy the will of the monastic, nor does he attempt to subdue it to his own arbitrary will; instead he undertakes the heavy burden of the sacred responsibility, and for that he becomes an associate of God in His divine task of human creation. Sometimes, an elder physically not strong enough, might need the services of the candidate, but that act doesn't alter the essential quality of monastic obedience. If the abbot and the other fathers of the monastery are sometimes obliged to turn to "discipline" and to force their brothers, that is a clear sign of the fall of monasticism and possibly a total loss of its purpose and its essence.

In reality, the issue of obedience is closely related to the problem of choosing a spiritual guide, meaning an elder. But, let's leave this aside so that we don't make our text too heavy. It's enough to mention what Saint Symeon the new Theologian, and other Fathers have left us about how the one who honestly, humbly and with many prayers seeks a guide, he will eventually find one. "Ask and you shall find", says

Christ (Mat. 6:7).

The matter of obedience is never ending. But, the basic principle remains the same: Do not trust yourself. This is especially useful for those just beginning, but even monks who have matured in the spiritual fight, never abandon obedience.

It is necessary to commence any action by asking for a blessing, to give to any endeavor of us the character of a divine project. All unimportant matters of everyday life as well as the important ones demand the knowledge of God's will, because in human existence all things matter. With this blessing, life as a whole obtains a holy dimension, as only what has been fulfilled "in the name of the Lord" is written in eternity. Christ said: "Every plant that my heavenly Father has not planted will be pulled up by the roots." (Mat. 15:13). With obedience, eternal life becomes reality here and now. The obedient monastic feels the presence of the spirit of God which gifts to the soul not only a deep peace, but also the feeling of passing "from death to life" (John 5:24).

Virginity and purity constitute the second basic monastic promise. The meaning of purity as a way of life in the image of Jesus Christ is in a strange way so very little accepted in the world today (even the Christian one), that we must particularly stress out the dogmatic base of this promise. The millennial experience of the Church has proven beyond any reasonable doubt that the exclusion of sexual function not only does not cause any sort of mental or physical damage but in the contrary, when practiced correctly it increases a person's physical stamina as well as longevity and mental health, while at the same time also contributes to the spiritual development of the person.

During the last years many scientific works have confirmed the spiritual fruition of what modern psychology calls "immaterial purity". One can only rejoice for this statement of fact. Throughout the centuries, monastic celibacy never stopped being perverted or even been rejected as a pathological phenomenon that goes "against nature". Modern scientific experience in this field is still quite insignificant to be compared to the long lasting experience of the Church or to be able to enrich it, so it's of little importance to the monks.

Setting aside any detailed examination of the dogmatic and anthropological side of the problem, allow me just to note that, for us, the basic and undisputed vindication of this promise (to which all other proof leads to) is found inside the "model" given to us by Christ Himself. "I have set you an example that you should do as I have done for you." (John 13:15). Only an insane person would risk to say that the life of Christ was against nature. We as Christians face only one ultimate challenge: To become like Christ in everything, so that through this similarity to Christ the Man, to achieve similarity to God which is the final cause and meaning of our existence. Saint Barsanuphius says that obedience "leads to heaven and transforms those who acquired it similar to the Son of God". But the same can be said about virginity and chastity. According to the opinion of Saint Methodius of Olympus as expressed in his work "Symposium of the Ten Virgins", a book summarizing the views of the ancient Church about celibacy, one can only achieve the "by image" of God by employing and revealing in his human existence the image that was revealed to us from Christ. We see the Church constantly teaching salvation through the lens of divinity. But where should we search for a trustworthy criterion in order to be able to "see and feel?" (A' John 1:1). Surely, only through our likeness to the "God was manifest in the flesh" (A' Tim. 3:16) we become like God, like His unearthly and eternal existence. This has always been the approach of the Church since the early days of its existence, regarding this matter. This is reflected inside the letters, the texts of holy sermons[14], and inside the great writings of the Fathers. Allow me to quote excerpts from a couple of them.

Inside the first of the two "Letters to the Virgins" attributed to Saint Clement of Rome, we read (in the sixth chapter): "The womb of the Virgin was the one that gave birth to the Son of God our Lord Jesus Christ. And the body our Lord wore and with which He completed His struggle "in this world" he took from the Holy Virgin. From this, we realize the majesty and the glory of virginity. Do you wish to become a Christian? Mimic Christ in everything. Saint John was an angel "sent before" and no prophet "born by a woman" was ever greater than him. And

---

14 "For this reason the unreachable God became human, to pull us to the heights" The Akathist Hymn, Eighteenth House.

that angel of the Lord was a virgin. Another John, the one that “leant on the chest of the Lord” the one who loved Him the most, was also a Saint[15]. This explains the fact that the Lord loved him so much. After them, Paul, Barnabas, Timothy, and others appeared “whose names were in the book of life”. They all loved this kind of sanctity and continued to be in a state of “sanctity” until the end of their ascetic lives, proving that they are real emulators of Christ and Sons of the living God” because “those who resemble Christ are completely like Him[16]”.

In his book “About the garment of the Virgins”, Saint Kyprianos of Cartage when speaking about the value of chastity says: “The Virgins are the blossoms of the Church, the glory and the decoration of spiritual grace; work of praise and honor, full and incorruptible, image of God that correlates to the sanctity of the Lord, the most glorious members of Christ’s flock, and as chastity increases, so does the joy of the mother Church.”

In his book “Symposium of the ten Virgins” Saint Methodius of Olympus refers to chastity as a “particularly great work”; like a “mystery”. And without a doubt, if marriage is a mystery, chastity is

---

[15] From the context here, it is obvious that the words “Saint” and “sanctity” –three lines below- refer to ‘the virgin’ and the ‘state of virginity’.

[16] 3rd century text translated and saved as “Mgr Clément Villecourt, Les deux Epîtres aux Vierges de Saint Clément romain, Paris 1855, ch. 6, p. 131-133.

also one.

Virginity and chastity in the Christian sense is fundamentally different to what non-Christians and many others comprehend today by hearing these words. The meaning of virginity and chastity are related, but are not the same. During the tonsure, those who come to monasticism after being married (or having extramarital relations) recite the promise of chastity, meaning full abstinence in the future, while those who never had sexual contact recite the promise of virginity.

Purity-prudence, as the words reveal means integrity or full wisdom. For the Church, this meaning includes not only dominion over sexual urges or the conviction of the flesh in general and by this "victory over nature", but the acquisition of the combination of perfections that are worthy of prudence and whose expression is the stable existence "in God" by all intellect and all heart. In its fullest actualization, the ascetic accomplishment of chastity can restore the person in spirit to its virgin state. The Holy Fathers indeed consider real virginity as a supernatural condition. In its perfect form is considered an uninterrupted residence "inside God's love", like an actualization of Christ's command to love God "with all your heart, all your soul, and with all the strength and intelligence". Under the light of this standard, any deviation of the mind and the heart away from the love of God is viewed as spiritual "adultery", thus a violation of divine love.

Virginity is not a naïve ignorance of our

biological realities. The highest and most unique example of perfection we have, the Virgin Mary, responded to the Angel bringing the news that she will give birth to the Son by asking this: "how will this happen to me without knowing a man?" (Luke 10:31).

Complete biological chastity is not necessarily, virginity. One of our biggest Saints, Basil of Caesarea said bitterly about himself: "I have met no woman, and I am not a virgin". Indeed, he who hasn't committed a sexual act, but is occupied by it in his imagination, is no longer a virgin.

Besides the sexual act there are also many forms of corruption and self-corruption; forms the Church forbids describing them further to avoid strengthening any image of sin into the mind of the writer or the reader.

The Church realizes there are three spiritual states for humanity: The supernatural, the natural, and the one against nature, or abnormal state. Virginity and ascetic purity understood as gifts from Grace belong to the first state. In the second, we have marriage which is blessed as a mystery. In the third, any other sort of sexual life which would be spiritually against nature, or abnormal. The Fathers say: "Do not attempt what is supernatural so that you don't fall to the unnatural". From this comes the rule that no one is allowed to enter the monastic life without a preliminary period of testing. The monk who does not hold his chastity is placed much lower than a man who is bonded in a pious marriage, which the Church recognizes as a path to salvation. Since the monastic who has given the promise of purity is being denied the right of marriage that is blessed by the Church, any deviation from him regarding their purity is considered a fall, a fall actually into an unnatural state. The normal temperate marriage maintains the physical and moral health of an individual, while any other sort of sexual life even if it only manifests in the form of voyeurism, has a disintegrating result to the person as a whole, mentally and physically alike. This disintegrating activity is especially strong against the monastic who sins in that way and breaks the promises they made in front of God. The internal conflict that is born inside of them as a result of the loss of grace takes an immeasurably larger character, and the suffering from guilt can reach the state of dark despair. For one to imagine relations of the flesh in the absence of a normal biological act, has led in many cases to serious mental illnesses and even to complete madness. Psychiatrists can attest to the frequency of such cases[17].

---

[17] In his book "The Symposium of the Ten Virgins', Saint Methodius of Olympus describes among others that the consciousness of humanity was developed when it was cultivated spiritually inside the knowledge of the most perfect ways of living, of virginity, and of purity. This historic evolution advanced through the following stages: In the beginning, "when the earth was not filled with people" because it was necessary for humanity to be fruitful and multiply, men were marrying their sisters. Later, as the human race had multiplied and spread on the earth, Divine Providence through the teachings of

the Prophets, delivered humankind from that way of life into something ethically superior as the wedding with a sister was considered "incestuous". Then, the ideal of monogamy appears "that we must not mate with many like animals and be born like them for fornication", also, "that we must not be adulterers". Later on, Christianity started teaching people an even higher perception of life, and the Church introduced a new restriction to marriage according to the level of spiritual affinity. Two brothers for example, cannot be married to two sisters, and so on, something that even today is incomprehensible outside our Church. The teachings of the Apostles led to the perceptions first of the "honest marriage" and of the "spotless bed", and finally to Christian chastity which is a "teaching to elevate one above the flesh and enter the safe harbor of incorruptibility" …

At this point, I would like to make a remark about the unusual relativity of the sermon regarding celibacy and purity in our days. The break of the bondage of marriage as it has been established by the Church (as well as any violation turning against it), not only humiliates the human way of life, but brings more, worse things; the personality disintegration of the one committing the sin, the collapse of families, the disintegration of kingdoms, and the destruction and loss of entire countries and populations. In relation to that, it must be said that if the spiritual evolution of humankind continued according to the directions Saint Methodius suggested, one of the most important and worrying problems of our days, the overpopulation of our planet, could find a solution truly worthy to the human as "son of God". The savage theories that regulate populations through image of Christ the perfect human cannot be founded on the rejection of a sexual life, or the deprecation of marriage which is blessed by God and the Church, the deprecation or damnation of the act through which "the person is born into the world" (John 16:21). In its Synodic decisions, the Church rejects those who resort to monasticism because they despise marriage or they belittle marriage because of pride. That's why the Fathers tested any person who wanted to be a monastic, to find out if they had a real calling towards it. There are several ranks of calling. There are those who receive grace so abundantly that even their intellect and their bodies feel they have been sanctified. For these people, complete abstinence from carnal life becomes a necessity, not only as far as physical acts but also as far as thoughts are concerned, even when they are sleeping. A lower rank exists when the soul just longs for chastity, intellect tends towards purity, and an internal desire for dedication pushes carnal thoughts aside. Many enter monastic life being in that state which despite the fact it is less certain than the first one, it also constitutes a positive "higher" calling.

Many years of experience have shown that a love for God is strong inside marriage, but it's a love less fiery. When love for God passes a certain limit and gains more strength, the soul instinctively tends to move away from anything that is not in harmony with the love it feels. It's not my task to find a logical

---

mutual destructive wars would not be tolerated anymore and life on earth could really be "as in Heaven, Your Kingdom come".

explanation to this noteworthy phenomenon of religious psychology that repeats through the centuries in remarkable frequency. Maybe it doesn't even fall into the jurisdiction of logical definitions. I base this view of mine on the works of the Holy Fathers, as well as on the observations I've made as a confessor. From many discussions I have had with ascetics I have come to the solid conclusion that when the soul reaches knowledge through a real experience of the love of Christ, the sweetness of this love gives birth to an irresistible attraction towards God, an uninterruptable thirst for Him, and at the same time a deep sympathy towards the world. A consequence of this situation is the effortless and let's say natural separation from the pleasures of the flesh that freeze and extinguish the Divine love. The very nature of great love towards Christ is such, that does not tolerate any demotion to carnal pleasures in general, and even less to sexual pleasures that create the strongest of all things earthly, impression on the soul. The intellect under the energy of the love of God is stripped of all earthly things and rejects all images. I know there are many who hold completely different opinions, but aren't the words "My Spirit shall not abide in man forever, for he is flesh" (Gen, 6:3), talking about them?

Experience itself shows to the ascetic how the sensual pleasure of any kind whether it comes from the eye, or from the taste, the ear, the touch, or the smell, prevents the soul from reaching whatever is immeasurably higher and more valuable, and deprives him of the assurance of the prayer; on the other hand, physical pain many times helps to cleanse the intellect and elevate in contemplation.

When purity itself becomes a deep need of the spirit, then it leads naturally to what is called "strictness" or life of asceticism. Anything not completely essential for our existence, is put aside to give the spirit the greatest possible freedom for contemplation. If food and sleep were not absolutely needed for our physical existence (like tobacco and drugs that are not), the champion of purity would never touch food, or give "sleep to his eyes" (Psalms 134:4) in order to dedicate their entire strength of their intellect towards the thought of God and prayer.

Sin doesn't reside in any physical human function, but in the passions. The Holy Great Shepherd said: "We do not kill the body we kill the passion". The Orthodox ascetic does not fight against the body but against the passions and the "cunning spirits that exist between the earth and the skies" (Ephes. 6:12), because it's not the body that distances us from God, the body has been called to become "temple of the Holy Spirit inside of us" (A' Kor. 6:19), but the passions and their pleasures.

The Orthodox ascetic life is based on the dogmatic consciousness that the life of a logical being is formed by the union between two wills, two energies: the Divine, and the human. Because of this fact, celibacy and chastity are not just a gift from grace but also a consequence of a logical effort. Each gift from Grace in this world then, unavoidably entails a great struggle in order to prudently safe keep it, a spiritual "accomplishment". What grace teaches when present inside a person, the person must preserve when grace appears to be absent. The person must continue living as if grace is still present. This is the beginning of willful discipline, the ascetic education. In his study “About Virginity”, Saint Gregory of Nyssa expresses himself like this: “The spiritual accomplishment of chastity is an art and strength of divine life, which teaches those who live in the flesh to emulate towards the incorporeal nature”. This happens when the person acts by his or her own will and reason, therefore keeping one’s chastity and integrity becomes an act of ascetic cultivation and art. It is not my purpose at this moment to develop further on this topic. Just allow me to mention that the most vital part of this “art” is the “maintenance of the nous”; the most important principle of this achievement is to “not surrender the nous”. If this fails, no training of the body will achieve its purpose, while an ascetically trained intellect can maintain not only its own purity and freedom, but also the peace of the body even under circumstances that to others might seem impossible to realize.

Again, I repeat for the sake of emphasising it, that the Orthodox Church is fully conscious of the unique character of this call. Its knowledge comes not just from experience, but also from the words of Christ Himself who said “Not everyone can accept this word, but only those to whom it has been given.” (Mat. 19:11). From this comes the careful preliminary examination of those who ask to make the monastic promises. From this comes the reluctance to put single clerics in worldly communities, with some rare exceptions that most of the times are forced by circumstances. In this we also see the respect of the Church towards marriage which is held in such a high and esteemed place that is not considered an obstacle even to the performance of the Sacrament of Holy Communion[18].

The great Saint John Climacus ends the wonderful chapter about chastity with the following words: "Been in flesh and having received the gift of purity, he has seen a prologue of his death, his resurrection, and of the future imperishable life".

The third fundamental promise, the one of owning nothing known also as the promise of poverty, complements in a natural way the first two and with them constitutes an insoluble unity for the achievement of pure prayer and at the same time a more perfect identification with God through likeness with Christ who had so little interest in material possessions that He "has no place to lay his head." (Mat. 8:20). Experience shows to people that to reach pure prayer[19] it's necessary to release the intellect from the images of material things that burden it.

---

[18] Saint Pafnutius who was himself celibate, during the First Council of Nicaea, according to the testament of Sozomen, was fiercely in favor of marriage which he refused to consider as an obstacle towards the priesthood. Of the numerous decisions made during the Councils mentioning this issue, we can particularly mention the 13th Canon of the 6th Ecumenical Council which categorically rejects the Roman habit of not accepting married men into priesthood.

[19] Referring to the Jesus prayer of the heart.

The monastic promise to renounce the spirit of holding property stresses the struggle against the passions of greed, stinginess, and love for material possessions. The monk doesn't promise to live "poor", rather he promises to release his spirit from the desire of "possessions". The point of success here is the appearance of a very strong desire of "not owning" to a point where the true ascetic does not spare even their own body. This is the only way that makes it possible to live a truly majestic spiritual life.

At first someone will argue: "How can I free myself completely from the things of this world? Since I have a body, I am myself a material thing and the life of this body of mine is inevitably connected to matter. Do all of the above mean that I have to leave myself to die?" No, things are not like this. The wise ascetic effort focuses on reduction to a minimal point of material needs, without which it would be impossible for one to live. But the measure of those needs is different every time[20].

The modern man hasn't acquired the ability to organize his life in such a way that allows him to have enough time for prayer as well as for the spiritual viewing of God. The cause of this is greed, the passion that Apostle Paul calls "idolatry" (Colos. 3:5) and Saint John Climacus "daughter of infidelity, blasphemy against the Gospel, distancing from God". True Christian poverty is unknown and

---

[20] Compare the above to the teachings of the Saint Synklytiki who we meet in the text about her life written by Athanasius of Alexandria.

incomprehensible to the world. And if we continue and say that this spirit of lack of ownership increases and develops to the point where it embraces not only the material but also "intellectual" possessions, to the majority of people it will sound insane. People consider their education as spiritual wealth without suspecting the existence of a knowledge far superior, of a wealth truly unmatched because it brings along a deep peace. By going after material comforts people have lost their spiritual comfort. The materialistic drive that prevails in our era is acquiring in a fast pace - a demonic character. This is nothing more than the expression of the dynamics of sin.

The love for possessions exiles the love for God and for our fellow man. People can't see this, and don't want to understand that their illicit desires are the source of the whole world's sufferings. Saint John Climacus says "The love for money is called 'the root of all evils'" (A' Tim. 6:10) and that's the truth indeed as love for money is the source of theft, envy, separation, hostility, cruelty, hatred, murder, and war".

So, to free ourselves from the slavery of petty cares, to cleanse our intellect and allow our spirit to enjoy a freedom truly majestic or to be more precise, a freedom similar to the freedom of God, renunciation is essential also here, because as Saint John Climacus mentions: "the poor man, in prayer is clean". He who has tasted the above, happily despises the below, indigent monk bishop of the world, indigent worker, his skills are considered as nonexistent" and, when he possesses nothing he is not sad, but keeps on living as if he does own something.

With the hope that this concise report of the fundamental monastic promises has helped the reader to understand up to a point, the essence of the Orthodox ascetic life, I would like in order to complete the image of monasticism and exclude any possibility of misunderstanding to add a few words from the promise of, "will you remain in the Monastery and in ascesis up to your last breath?" which constitutes the first question in the "Small Schema", and the second in the "Great Schema".

The candidate here is asked two questions combined into one: If they will "remain in the monastery" and if they will "remain in ascesis". The first one is not a sacrosanct part of monasticism like the rest of the promises. Monastic life can be experienced outside the monastery, in the desert as well as in the world. In the biographies of many Saints which were also monastics, we read about the voluntary or involuntary abandonment of the monastery in which they gave their promises, without this being considered a "fall" or even a violation of their monastic status. Many of them were taken away from their monasteries and were placed somewhere, in order to perform an hierarchical service within the Church. Many, for different reasons moved to other monasteries, many received the blessing of their superiors and then departed pursuing a noble cause. Finally, there are examples of those who left a monastery due to the "difficulty of salvation" that existed inside it.

When monastic promises are made outside a monastery, this question is usually skipped, leaving only the second part about the life of "ascesis" until the monk's last breath. It is though, a completely natural question to ask and will always remain an integral part of the tonsure, since whoever is accepted in the community becomes a co-owner of everything belonging to the monastery, and a shareholder in the fullness of the material and the spiritual life of the monastery. The brothers who accept a new member in their spiritual family naturally expect a promise of faith from his part, so that the elders can trust him and count on him for all things to come.

The second part of the question about remaining "in ascesis" until someone's last breath gives to the monastic promises of an irrevocable and inexorable character that spans beyond the limits of this temporary life. The Lord said: "No one who puts his hand to the plow and looks back is fit for the kingdom of God." (Luke 9:62).

Truly, for one to keep monastic promises for a specific time period only, it is as if they don't understand the true meaning and they transform them into a simple exercise of devoutness, while in reality they signify the abandonment of spiritual infancy and the transition to maturity. Apostle Paul says: "When I was a child, I talked like a child, I thought like a child, I reasoned like a child. When I became a man, I put the ways of childhood behind me." (A' Cor. 13:11). Childhood cannot be regained not so much in regards to time, as in a sense of quality of life. How can experience, knowledge, and intelligence disappear? In a similar manner, these promises express another side of existence, of its meaning, its purpose and content. What separates, for example, the promise of chastity from a temporary temperance on behalf of anyone, since it will be considered as an ephemeral exercise? What if we consider obedience as a temporary exercise, where is the consciousness then that through obedience we fight against the crushing narrowness of the "self will" and the ego, in order to become carriers of the will of our heavenly Father? In a similar fashion, if someone views poverty only as a temporary state of deprivation, where is our perception that this promise symbolizes our decision to tame with the help of God the power of the matter seeking to impose itself over the spirit? Thus, the one who breaks the promises he has given is not "suitable" for the Kingdom. And we must say here, that if a monk forgoes his promises, this generally means that he has made them without understanding them as he should, or without being in the proper spiritual disposition. In other words, he didn't keep his promises because he made them frivolously.

We started examining the three ways of calling, the three renunciations, the three sides of the cross, and the three ranks of monasticism. But Gregory of Nazianzus adds another teaching regarding the three births through which the person must pass during his life. In a letter written in a poetic form addressed to "Saint Vitale on behalf of his sons" he writes: "With the first birth of flesh and blood the person arrives to earth and disappears quickly; then the second birth 'by Holy Spirit' comes when the light from above descends on him as long as he has been washed by the water (of baptism). The third (birth) through tears and pains cleanses the image (of God) within us, which has been smudged by evil. The first of these (births) comes from our parents, the second from God, but for the third one we are the cause, appearing in the world as a beneficial light".

From the above we understand that the last birth is the most perfect one. The person, after receiving the gift of grace which has illuminated for him both the life divine, and his own fall, he is attached (without a chance of being withdrawn) through a diligent effort, to good. It is this conscious decision of choice and attachment to the divine that constitutes the core of the Christian ascetic life. The symptoms of this condition are a deep lack of satisfaction of the spirit from all that exists on earth, a "nostalgia" of God, a desire for God, and a passionate search for God.

This is, I think, expressed in the words of Saint Silouanos:

> "My soul longs for the Lord, and I seek Him in tears.
> How could I not seek You?
> Since You first have searched for me, and allowed me to rejoice by Your Holy Spirit,
> And my soul loved You!."

www.ingramcontent.com/pod-product-compliance
Ingram Content Group UK Ltd.
Pitfield, Milton Keynes, MK11 3LW, UK
UKHW021934190726
13853UKWH00004B/1432

9 798589 619720